THE GIPSY VIOLIN

ALBUM OF
WORLD-FAMOUS GIPSY ROMANCES

ARRANGED FOR
VIOLIN AND PIANO

EDITED AND REVISED BY
W. RUSS-BOVELINO

✦

T0156376

CONTENTS

✦

TWO GUITARS

Russian Song

SLOWLY FLOWS THE RIVER MAROS
(Maros vize)

Hungarian Gipsy Song

DEEP SORROW

Gipsy Air

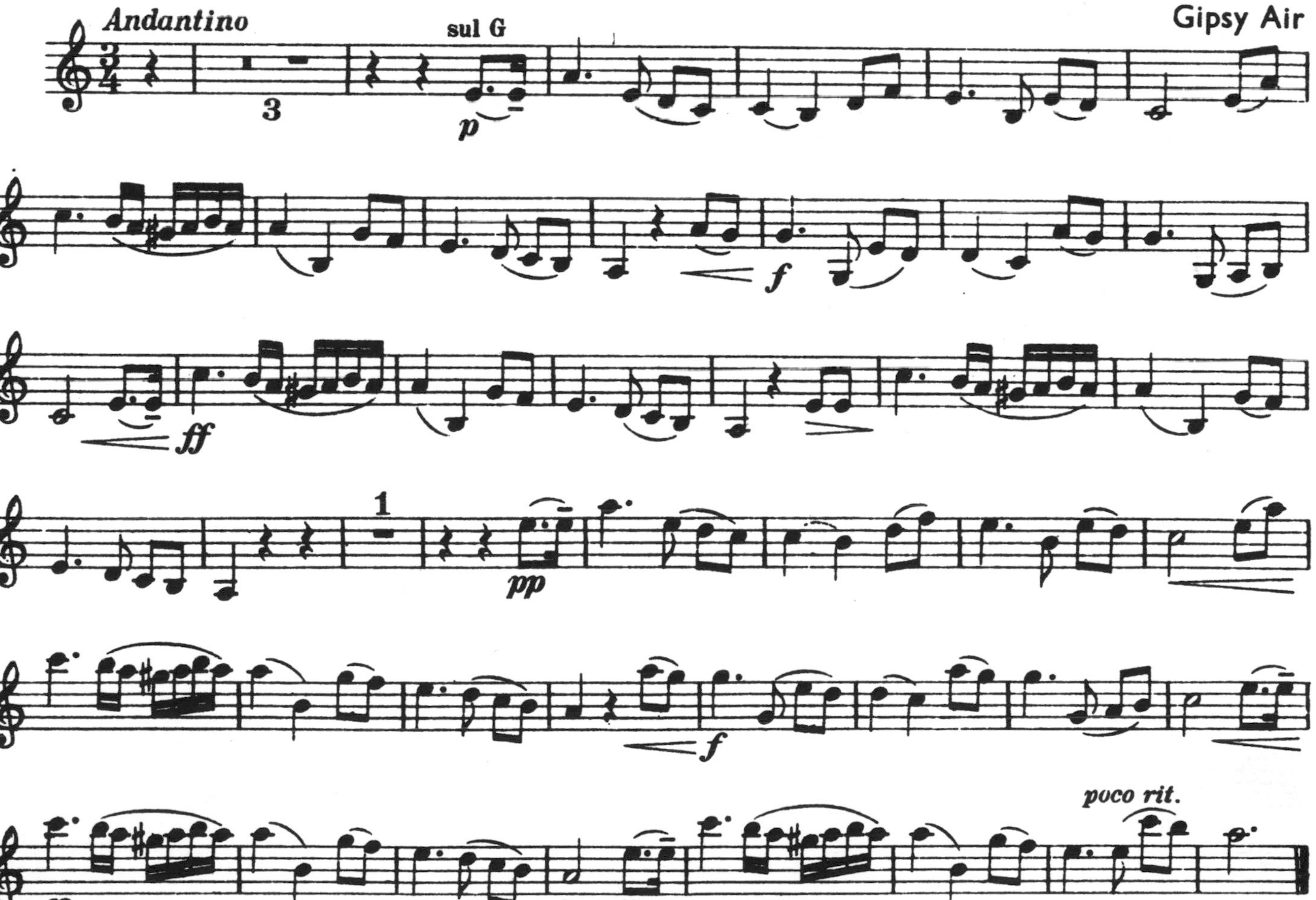

Made in England *Tous droits d'exécution réservés*
Imprimé en Angleterre

GOLDEN WHEAT
(Ritka buza)

Czárdás

THE SLEIGH RIDE
(Repül a szan)

Hungarian Romance

4

DON'T LEAVE ME
(Nu m'abandona)

Gipsy Romance

Made in England   *Tous droits d'exécution réservés*
Imprimé en Angleterre

HUNGARIAN FANTASY

Wolfgang Russ-Bovelino

100 KISSES I'LL STEAL FROM YOU
(Tiz par csokot)

Hungarian Air

BLACK EYES

Russian Gipsy Romance

Made in England
Imprimé en Angleterre

Tous droits d'exécution réservés

RASPOSCHOL

Russian Gipsy Air

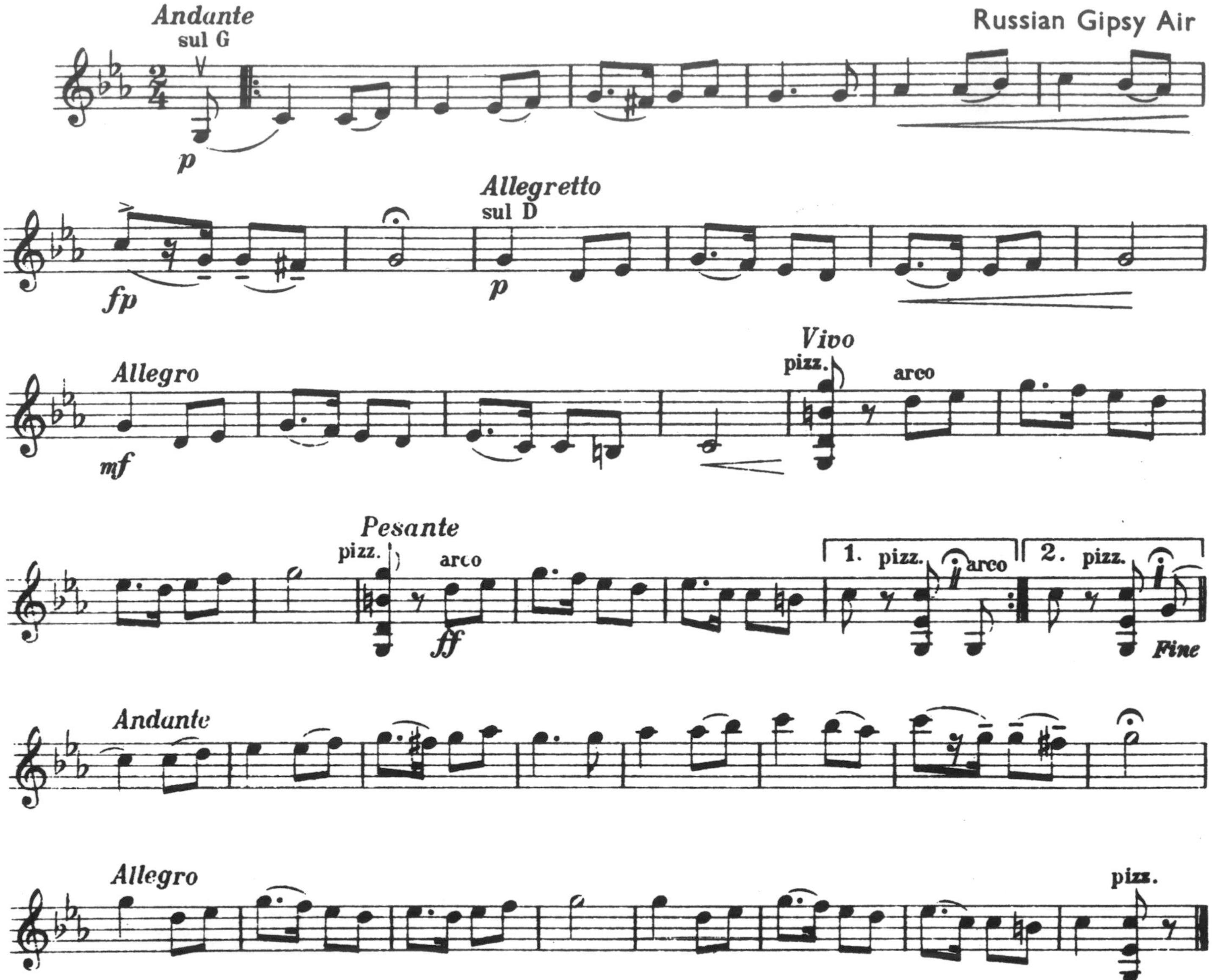

D.C. al Fine

LAVOTTA

Hungarian Serenade

Made in England
Imprimé en Angleterre

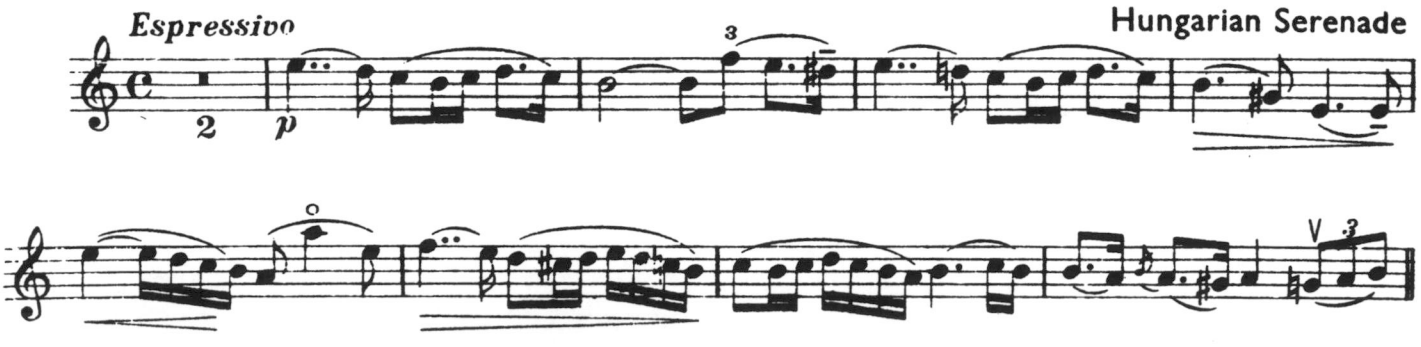

ONE KITTEN, TWO KITTENS
(Egy cica, két cica)

Hungarian Song

HEISSA TROIKA

Russian Gipsy Waltz

THE STARS IN THE SKY
(Nincsen, annyi tenger csillag)

Somewhat moderato Hungarian Gipsy Air

WIND, TELL MY SWEETHEART
(Suga a fülébe)

Slowly Gipsy Song

GIPSY AIR

KURT STEINER
arranged by Leop. Kubanek

SINAI HORA

Rumanian Dance

Made in England
Imprimé en Angleterre

Tous droits d'exécution réserves